A Celebration of the Avon Ne

C000075627

Coordinator and Compiler: Katie White

Design and editing: Katie White and Roy Gallop

History and Development research: Glyn Williams, Roy Gallop, Christine Hodgson
Anton Bantock, Sue Stops and Ingrid Skeels

Copy writer: Ingrid Skeels
William Jessop: Katie White
I.K.Brunel: Geoffrey Body
Bridges & Churches: Kathy Derrick, Katie White and Phil Draper
Geology: Peter Andressen
Mud: Tess Green
Flora and Fauna: Members of Friends of the Avon New Cut
The Future of the New Cut: Tess Green and John Purkiss

Fiducia Press 2006
ISBN 0 946217 23 8

Printed in Great Britain by Doveton Press
This book is a project of the Southville Community Development Association

Contents

Langton St Bridge

Introduction

Every day, thousands of people cross the Avon New Cut for work or pleasure. They walk, drive or cycle along its banks and look across it to Spike Island, the Docks, or Hotwells and Clifton beyond. Many people are aware that they are crossing a tidal river: sometimes they see a brimming flood and sometimes just a trickle of water flowing between muddy banks. However few people realise that 200 years ago, this waterway was not even here; that it was man-made between 1804 and 1809, dug out by labourers using just pick, shovel, wheel barrow and gun powder.

The creation of the New Cut was an incredible achievement. It was a feat of engineering and hard manual labour, carried out to try and secure Bristol's position as an important but diminishing British and international dock and harbour. Originally the River Avon ran through the city and Bristol's docks and harbour were tidal and difficult to navigate. At low tide, ships were stranded on the mud with their hulls drying out and loading and unloading were extremely difficult. Because of these problems, Bristol began to lose important trade to easier, more accessible harbours. The aim of the New Cut was to vastly improve the harbour by re-routing the tidal part of the river and closing off the docks with dams and locks. Doing this would create an area with a constant water level: a 'wet dock' or 'floating harbour'. Ships would then be able to enter, load and unload far more safely and efficiently.

This book is a celebration of the two hundredth anniversary of the Avon New Cut. We want to tell the story of the New Cut: What was Bristol like before it was created? How did the New Cut change the city? How was it built and what is its future?

In telling this story, we would like to stop and look at particular features of the Cut: the key people who made and improved it including, of course, Isambard Kingdom Brunel; the trade and industry that grew and died along its banks; the bridges and ferries that cross it; the churches that stand by it; and the geology, mud, flora and fauna of this incredible man-made channel. By bringing together facts, local history, maps, images and drawings, we want to explore the creation and evolution of something that changed Bristol's geography and history forever, as well as the local areas of Ashton, Bedminster and Southville.

Today, Bristol is no longer the important trading centre and harbour that it once was and most of the old industries are long gone. The Cut, however, is no less vital to the city and Docks than when it was built. Allowing a safe harbour for sport, leisure and recreational craft, as well as safeguarding the waterside as an attractive centre for the city of Bristol, it is a beautiful and vibrant place in which to live and work. The Cut is also much more than this however. It is a rich seam of history, running close to where we live, full of echoes and marks from the past; and it is a wonderful wildlife habitat, rich in flora and fauna, bringing the countryside into the heart of the city.

We hope that, whether you are walking along it or crossing over it, you will begin to explore, enjoy and value the Avon New Cut.

Bristol Before the New Cut

The Early Harbour

There has probably been some form of port at Bristol for over a thousand years. The area was certainly settled before 1000BC, as remains have been found of Bronze Age burial mounds and Iron Age hill forts in different parts of Bristol. Many pre-historians also believe that the blue stones of Stonehenge were rafted up the River Avon on their journey from Preseli in West Wales to the Salisbury Plain.

Around 40AD, Roman settlers built the first known harbour at a place called Abona, now Sea Mills, using it to bring in supplies for trade and war to their nearby town of Aquae Sulis, or Bath, as we know it today.

Bristol itself is first recorded in the Anglo Saxon Chronicle of 1051, its name being 'Brigstowe', meaning 'place by the bridge'. The Saxon town had grown up in the area now known as Castle Park, on the high ground close to the junction of the rivers Frome and Avon. The settlement developed close to a wooden bridge that spanned the Avon (in the spot where today's Bristol Bridge is to be found), linking the two lands of Mercia and Wessex. Here, the town was safe from the high tidal range of the Avon, which is one of the greatest in the world. On the highest tides, the difference in water levels can grow to nearly 40 feet.

From early on, Bristol was a very successful trading centre, due mainly to its geographical position at the junction of three main trading routes: the Avon, the Severn and the Wye. The town also had easy access to the Southwest, Wales and the Midlands. During the 11th and 12th centuries, Bristol ships were engaged in

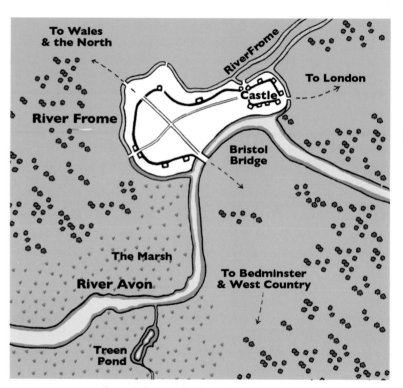

Bristol during the late Saxon period.

4

trade with Dublin, Wales and the Somerset and Devon coastal towns, making it one of the wealthiest towns in the country.

Early Civil Engineering

By the year 1200, Bristol was a thriving mercantile town with a population of nearly 2000. Boats sailed right up to Bristol Bridge and unloaded their cargo on both sides of the river. This was the earliest point in the history of Bristol's harbour when there was not enough wharf space to cope with the traffic.

In the 1240s, Bristol's first great engineering works were carried out, transforming the harbour and its use for the next five hundred years. To begin with, the river Avon was temporarily dammed and diverted around Bristol Bridge, so that the old wooden structure could be replaced with a fine, new stone bridge. Then, more ambitiously and as a precursor of things to come, another scheme diverted the river Frome into a permanent new cut of about 750 yards long. While the Frome used to curve round and join the Avon close to Bristol Bridge, it now followed a new man-made route and joined the Avon further down. New quays were formed – Narrow Quay and Broad Quay – increasing mooring space and doubling the number of ships that the port could service at any one time. (Today, only Narrow Quay can still be seen, between the Watershed and the Arnolfini; Broad Quay and the rest of the Frome have been covered over by the city centre.)

The excavation of this new length of riverbed was entirely manual and the work involved would have been staggering. The cost was £5000, putting the scheme in the same league as the

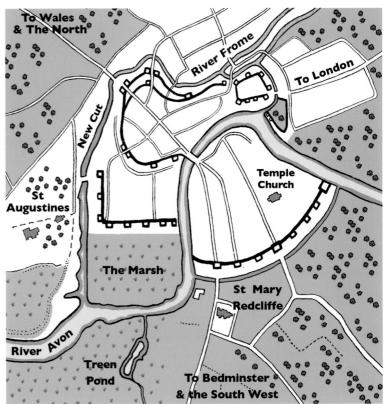

Bristol during the 13th Century showing the Frome River diverted to form a new cut with additional wharves for shipping.

great castles and cathedrals of the day. For the 13th century, this early new cut was a major civil engineering feat. It was, as Peter Aughton argues in his book Bristol, A People's History, "one of the greatest civil engineering works of the middle ages". It is unlikely that there was another town anywhere in the world which contained so much civil engineering activity."

The Growth of Bristol

The successful new developments allowed Bristol's maritime trade to grow still further and the Avon became a very busy waterway. By 1300 there were many regular sailings for Ireland, France, Spain and Portugal, as well as for many of the small

harbours along the Severn estuary. Bristol's main exports were rope, sailcloth, lead from the Mendip mines (a local material which can still be seen on the roof tops of cathedrals and castles across Europe) and cloth woven by local weavers in Redcliffe and made out of Cotswold wool. The town's main imports were hides, dried fish, corn, iron and - the most valuable import – wine, mainly from France.

By the end of the 14th century, Bristol's population had reached over 11,000 and the town had finally become a single administrative unit. Prior to this, Bristol had always been divided, the north half governed by Gloucestershire and the south half by Somerset. In 1373, Edward III granted a Royal charter so that the town "shall be a county by itself and be called the County of Bristol for ever…"

By now, trade had grown to include wine from Spain and Portugal and fish from as far away as the Icelandic coast. There was also still plenty of inland traffic: livestock, market produce, and wool for the town's growing woollen industry. Along the south bank of the Avon could be found shipbuilders, shipwrights, rope-makers, sail-makers and smiths. The harbour itself was busy with foreign ships, bringing in sailors from many different lands and returning Bristol sailors to their homes and families.

Bristol and the New World

By the 15th century, Bristolian merchants wanted to find new markets and for a while, Bristol was at the forefront of world exploration. In 1497, a merchant called John Cabot gained the backing of Henry VII to "find, discover, and investigate whatsoever islands, countries, regions or provinces… which before this time were unknown to all Christians." With 18 seamen on board, he set sail in his ship The Matthew (a replica of which is moored in the city docks today) and after several weeks of sailing, arrived at a new coastline – 'New Found Land' – where he planted the English flag. He was the first European to arrive on the American continent and his was the most important voyage to have set sail from the port of Bristol. However, he is often overlooked – even in Bristol itself – in favour of Columbus's more widely documented and publicised discovery of 1498.

After Cabot's voyage, Bristol Merchant Venturers continued in the exploration and mapping of the American continent. For example, a Bristol ship was sent to explore Virginia and its potential for agriculture and settlement; and a Bristol Quaker, William Penn, along with many of his Bristol brethren, formed the new colony of Pennsylvania, later to become a state. Bristol was really important in the early colonisation of America. Bristol faced west whilst London was an east coast port, so Bristol became the leading port for trade with the New World, further increasing the wealth and importance of the city. By the end of the 15th century, one wealthy merchant alone is recorded as owning 9 ships, ranging from 50 tons to 900 tons, and employing 800 men in the Bristol shipyards. Significant imports were now sugar, cork, olive oil, honey and woad (the latter for the Redcliffe dyers and weavers).

Local exports included soap, glass and pottery.

By the 17th century, Bristol's trade included something that, for a long time, Bristol preferred to forget: the trading of slaves. This was brought about by the demand for cheap labour to work the sugar and tobacco plantations in the New World. However this was not Bristol's first dealings with slavery. In the

A 16th century map of Bristol and the surrounding area.

11th century, Bristol sold and transported many English criminals and innocent people as slaves to Ireland.

Initially, Virginia was used as a penal colony and convicted criminals were spared the death sentence in England and shipped instead to work as slaves on the plantations. In 1651, for example, records show that 500 defeated Scots were transported after the Battle of Worcester. But by the end of the 17th century a new source of slaves had been found on the West African coast. From this time, the notorious 'triangular trade' developed between England, Africa and the New World of the Americas and Bristol became one of the busiest ports in the country. Cheap manufactured goods, such as metal pots and cotton cloth, were taken from Bristol to the African coast in exchange for people as slave labourers. The slaves were then transported in truly appalling conditions (chained and packed together with only 66 by 16 inches per slave in the hot, stinking hold of the ship) to America and the West Indies. There, if they survived the journey, the African slaves would be sold to work under harsh conditions on the plantations. Sugar, tea, rum, mahogany and tobacco were then brought back to Bristol where they filled the bonded warehouses along the sides of the city's docks. Merchants aimed to make a profit on each leg of the 'triangle'.

Second City to London

At the same time, trade also continued and grew with other countries, such as France, Spain and Portugal as well as towns closer to home such as Ludlow, Chepstow and Newport. Imports included coal for breweries and timber for shipbuilding and house building, to keep up with the rapid expansion of the city's population. Wealth poured into Bristol, much of it from the slave trade (which was also gathering much humanist opposition in Bristol itself). The city became a well-known manufacturing centre and one of England's leading industrial centres, with many industries lining the river banks of the Avon and Frome. From the end of the 17th century until almost the mid 18th century, the city and port were second only to London. As one visitor described it in 1793, Bristol had become "one of the finest mercantile havens in Europe".

The Harbour Reaches its Limits

The tides that had brought this wealth to Bristol Harbour, however, were also to play a key part in its initial decline.

From earliest times, the huge differences between high and low tide on the Avon meant that Bristol harbour was very difficult to navigate. In the 15th century, records describe how ships from many countries and regions would be moored in the Severn, waiting for the tide to turn so that they could sail into Bristol. As soon as the 'Black Rocks' were covered by the sea (a sign that the tide had turned enough), all the ships from "Spain, Portugal, Bordeaux, Bayonne, Gascony, Aquitaine, Brittany, Iceland, Ireland, Wales, and other parts" would weigh anchor and set sail for the town.

Over the centuries, as the number and size of ships going to and from Bristol continued to grow, this process became more and more difficult. For example by the 18th century, a large ship sailing up the Severn Estuary to reach the port of Bristol, would have travelled as follows. Firstly, the vessel would pick up a pilot off Lundy or Ilfracombe. On passing Flat Holm it would then enter the limit of the port. At King Road (off Portishead) a member of the customs team would board the ship and stay with it until it reached the quay. At Hungroad (near Pill), another anchorage would take place, where a post would indicate whether the tide was high enough to begin the safe passage into Bristol. A licence would then be obtained from the River Master to go ahead. If the boat was a large one, it would need towboats at this point (sometimes up to ten were used, carrying 100 men in total) to help it navigate the winding course and currents of the river. As ships grew larger and larger, this process became ever more difficult; the 'Horseshoe Bend' in the river near to Shirehampton becoming particularly difficult to navigate. Some ships were wrecked during the journey because they missed the tide or were carried onto the mud banks by the fast current; others were damaged by rocks and needed repairs.

Once in the harbour, difficulties for ships continued. The tidal nature of the river Avon meant that vessels were subject to drying out and wetting twice a day, which put a huge strain on their timbers as they lay in the mud at peculiar angles. One possible explanation for the expression "ship shape and Bristol fashion" comes from this, for if everything on board was not tidied neatly away, chaos would rule as the ship heeled over.

At the docks, ships were allowed to stay for between 17 and 20 weeks in order to unload and load. Taking on or discharging cargo was only possible when ships were upright around the top of the tide. As a result of all of these difficulties, there were often big delays in the movements of ships and also great overcrowding in the docks. Goods frequently rotted on board and the smell of the whole area in hot weather would have been unbearable.

Boats had to sit on the bottom in the mud at each low tide.

Bristol was also an expensive port. The Merchant Venturers, who controlled overseas trade in the city, collected all sorts of payments from traders, such as charges for anchorage, moorage, carriage, and upkeep of the lighthouses in the Bristol Channel and for the right to use the quays.

Not surprisingly, Bristol harbour started to lose trade to other ports and by the mid 18th century, its rival Liverpool had over-taken it. Liverpool had a large, deep waterfront; it was easily accessible to ships of the day; and the tidal range did not affect it. Charges in Liverpool were cheaper; ships could be unloaded and reloaded quickly, allowing the slave and trade ship owners to realise greater profit. Another crucial factor was the rise of the Lancashire cotton trade along with massive industrial development close to Liverpool and its docks. Once the northern canals were built, goods which had previously been sent to Bristol from the North Midlands down the River Severn, were now sent to Liverpool instead.

Despite Liverpool's ascendance in terms of sea trade, Bristol's businesses of sugar refining, glass making, tanneries, foundries and ship building continued to expand.

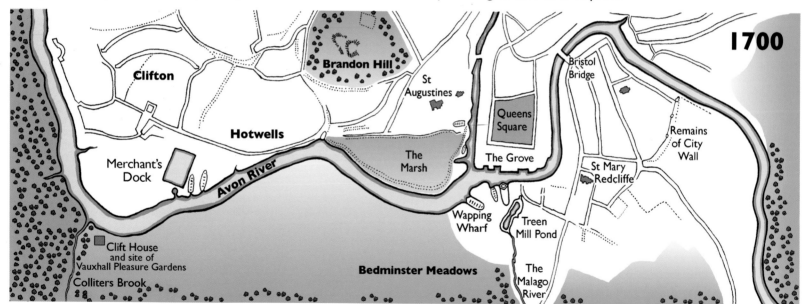

Early Attempts at a New Harbour

Although it had long been realised that the tidal nature of Bristol's harbour was causing problems for ships, it was some time before action was taken.

In 1712, a group of merchants built a dock at Sea Mills (where the old Roman port had been), in an attempt to shorten the difficult journey for ships. The dock was completed in 1717, but it was not the success that was hoped for, being too far from the city of Bristol. By 1779 it was completely derelict.

By this time, the City Council had formally recognised that there needed to be substantial changes to the docks. In 1758 they had advertised for surveys of the river to be carried out and measures for a 'wet dock' to be considered. A 'wet dock' is one which remains full of water, so that ships could stay afloat; cargo could easily be unloaded onto quays and the vessels quickly turned around. In 1764, the merchants launched a scheme to bring this about, but they could only raise a third of the cost.

Next, William Champion (a merchant, Quaker and anti-slavery protestor) built a dock at Rownham Meads, known as Merchant's Dock. It was a small dock, a tidal one, and not supported by the authorities who, if accounts are to be believed, preferred to spend their wealth on house building and high living, instead of improving the docks.

William Jessop's Scheme

In 1791, William Milton, the Vicar of Temple Church, put forward a scheme that involved developing a new river in Bristol that would take the tide away from the city's docks. The idea was taken up and developed by civil engineer William Jessop whose final plan was complex but brilliant.

Jessop agreed that the River Avon should be diverted away from the docks area through a new artificial river channel – or cut –

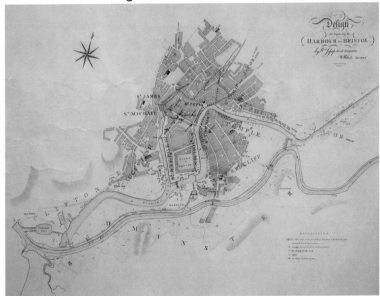

William Jessop's plan for the new floating harbour.

that would then join back to the original Avon. The old course of the river could then be used as a large, new dock, stretching from Hotwells to Temple Meads and covering an area of 70 acres; a permanent 'floating harbour', where water levels would remain constant.

To create this Floating Harbour, Jessop proposed that the New Cut would take the river from Totterdown to Rownham Ferry at Hotwells. A smaller cut, called the 'Feeder Canal', would connect the Avon with the new Floating Harbour and would be used by barges for inland navigational purposes. Two great locks would have to be constructed near Rownham Ferry and a large basin, the Cumberland Basin, would be built to house the ships inside the lock so that they could wait for the tide to carry them out to the Severn. Another Basin, Bathurst Basin, would be built at the point where the New Cut and the Floating Harbour would run very close to each other, at a place called Treen Mills in Bedminster. This would act as another possible entry point for smaller vessels, closer to the heart of the city. Swing bridges would also be needed at the Cumberland Basin so that dock and other traffic would be able to cross the water. Finally, to stop the harbour from silting up, there would have to be a controlled flow of water though the harbour and an overflow dam near the locks to carry this flow away and clear the silt.

The first response from the Council and the Merchant Venturers who controlled the wharfage along the old quays was to reject this scheme. They feared that boats would use the New Cut to escape their dock charges. However, the use of Bristol harbour was still

falling and the pressure to do something was immense. So Jessop's ambitious civil engineering scheme was finally approved in 1803 and the Bristol Docks Company was formed. The estimated cost was £300,000, including the price of the land.

Overfall Dam viewed at the start of the Avon New Cut from Ashton painting by T. L. Rowbottom.

The Creation of the Avon New Cut

The first stage of changing Bristol's docks and harbour involved excavating the bed of the new channel, which was to be named 'The Avon New Cut'. The first sod was cut at five o clock on the morning of May 1st 1804.

The excavation job was a huge one and involved, in parts, cutting deep into the solid rock to accommodate the volume of river water. As far as we know, the work was carried out entirely by 'Navvies': Irish, Scots and other itinerant labourers who travelled the land to work on the country's 'navigations' or canals. Story has

Irish Navvies breaking up the rock into blocks for use in the Cut masonary walls.

it that French prisoners of war were also used to do some of the digging, but there is no mention of this in any of the public records.

Just as when the Frome cut was dug nearly 600 years previously, the task was once again almost entirely a manual one, carried out by men using pick, shovel and wheel-barrow. Things had moved on to some extent since 1240 with the use of gunpowder to blast the rock and earth from the new canal. Early steam engines, a relatively new engineering development, were also used to shift vast quantities of rubble from the channel up to its banks.

In J P Malcolm's book of his travels around England between 1802 and 1805, Malcolm's First Impressions, he includes an account of a visit to Bristol in June 1805. He starts with an excursion to Dundry and then continues with a first hand account – the only first hand account - of watching work on the New Cut:

> "An unpleasant lane leads from the ferry to the verge of the new canal. As I passed this, a labourer advanced, and requested that I should return, as a person had at that instant fired the train of a ball of gunpowder, by means of which the work men loosen the otherwise immovable rocks of the site. In that instant the explosion occurred, and I saw a thousand splinters of various sizes hurled into the air, that as instantaneously fell, in a dangerous shower, in a circle probably 400 feet in diameter. The shock had not only rifted the rock immediately surrounding the powder, but huge fragments were removed from their beds and where wedges were driven into them. In this way they were made small enough to be raised by cranes by four men into carts which were

conveyed up the bank by operation of steam engines erected on the verge of the canal. The engines turned several wheels with strong chains round them, which by their revolutions lowered, emptied and raised the filled carts attached to the chains."

He goes on to note:

"Between the Bath Rd and Rownham Meads the variety of strata is interesting. Part consists of fine sand almost vermillion in colour, other of chocolate coloured rock, connected sometimes with a buff coloured rock. The latter cannot be broken without the use of gunpowder. There is also a lead coloured clay and gravel."

Malcolm records how none of the material brought up by the excavation was wasted:

"The excavations through rock have saved the proprietors a very considerable sum as the rock is used for the walls of the canal and cut perpendicular, serves as a wall for at least a quarter of a mile. The sand is admirably calculated for mixing mortar and the company had merely to burn their lime, which they were preparing to do on the spot when I saw the works. A temporary bridge erected with stone and intended mortar, crossed the canal at that time, but the fierce red of the sand in the latter ruined the appearance of the work. Iron bridges are however to be exclusively preferred".

Few other records exist of the excavation, though we do know that at one point in the digging of the Cut, workmen found a large quantity of trees about 20 ft down, embedded in clay, lying in one direction as if swept down suddenly in a gale. We also know that much of the spoil dug from the Cut was dumped on to the south bank of the new channel, as the surrounding land was quite marshy. This raised the bank on Coronation Road compared to the Cumberland Road side. This is most noticeable where Beauley Road and Greenway Bush Lane join Coronation Road.

At the time that the Cut was being dug, nearby Bedminster was still a very rural area, but the exploitation of the local coalfield, which had begun in 1745, was quickly changing it. Story has it that contractors would drive around to pay the Navvies' wages with gold in one corner of the horse trap, silver in another and a choice of refreshment in the other two corners. Many of the men frequented The Bull pub on North Street in Bedminster (a pub that is still there today, on the left just where North Street joins Dean Lane. It is currently called Bar Salt). Local people did not like the Irish Navvies much and there was often fighting in The Bull. After a particularly bad brawl, the press gang was called in and men were manhandled and marched away to work on the ships.

Work on the New Cut was finally completed in 1809. To commemorate its completion, the labourers were invited to a great dinner in a field opposite the Mardyke. They devoured "two oxen, roasted whole, a proportionate weight of potatoes and six hundredweight of plum pudding and one gallon of strong beer or 'sting' per guest". The English and the Irish, fuelled by such quantities of alcohol and the fact that they had long been on bad terms, ended up fighting again. Once more the press gang was called in, the leaders arrested and the brawl suppressed.

We have no record of the day when the water was first let into the New Cut, but it must have been an amazing moment for everyone who had been involved.

Throughout all of this time work had, of course, been going on to construct the Floating Harbour itself, the lock gates, Netham Weir,

Cumberland Basin and the Avon New Cut viewed from Rownham Hill 1825. Showing on the extreme right is Clift House. Ashton and Southville are still mainly a rural area. A painting by Samuel Jackson.

the Feeder Canal and, most importantly, the Overfall Dam which was to keep the water level in the harbour constant. Although by 1809 the main work was finished, the Cumberland Basin was not. Because of this, the first vessels entering the new floating harbour actually came up the New Cut and entered through the locks at Bathurst Basin. The total cost of the scheme was £600,000: twice the original estimate.

A Problem of Silt: Brunel's Solution

One element of Jessop's new harbour system was not very effective at all and it took another engineer to solve the problem. This is where Isambard Kingdom Brunel's engineering skills were first put into practice. When the New Cut was under construction, Brunel was still a baby, but by the 1830s he was a young man who had already submitted his design to the competition for the Clifton Suspension Bridge. He was a brilliant young engineer

Entrance to Bathurst Basin c1825 by Samuel Jackson.
To the left is the Bathurst Hotel and to the right the truncated spire of St Mary's Redcliffe Church and the chimney of John Acraman's iron works.

and his opinion was already greatly valued by the city. He was brought in as a consultant to look at the problems with the floating harbour.

The problem Brunel had to solve was one of silt. Like all rivers, the Avon and the Frome carried great quantities of silt in their waters. Before the New Cut, the movements of the tide had helped to carry the silt out to sea, along with the sewage and other waste that was discharged into the river from the city of Bristol.

The level of water in the Floating Harbour was kept constant by water coming in from the Frome River (joining at Narrow Quay) and the Feeder Canal. Excess water then flowed back into the New Cut via the 'Overfall' dam, which had a weir built into it. However, the system did not carry away sufficient amounts of silt to keep the harbour clear. On top of this, the sewage of practically the whole of Bristol was going into the Harbour and was no longer being taken out to sea.

The effect was not pleasant. Contemporary records describe it as "a very disagreeable and unwholesome effluvia", "particularly offensive to the eye" and "too loathsome to describe". When the tide came up it was actually worse, loaded with waste from sewers further down, and the stench was then "intolerable".

In 1817, George III's wife Queen Charlotte made a royal visit to Bristol and was trapped, breathing in the smell, when her coach got stuck on a bridge over the Frome, a great embarrassment for the city. In 1825 the Commissioners for Paving, Cleansing and Lighting took the Dock Company to Court about the issue.

In 1831-2 there was a terrible cholera epidemic in which 1,521 mainly poor people contracted the disease, many of them from the low-lying Bedminster area.

Temple Back etching by Dorothy E. G. Woollard c1915
This shows the upper part of the harbour beyond Bristol Bridge.

A little talked of civil engineer, William Shadwell Mylne, had already made one improvement. He had laid an underground culvert stretching from the Frome into the New Cut, taking the polluted river water to where the tides could carry it out to sea. This gave some relief to the people of the city, but not for those living south of the New Cut and it had not solved the main silting problem. Something significant still had to be done.

Brunel was the one to do this. He realised that, in order to take silt with it, excess water from the harbour needed to be taken from the bottom, rather than from the surface. In place of the Overfall, he constructed three shallow sluices and one deep scouring sluice between the harbour and the New Cut. He also designed a dredging vessel. This drag boat would scrape the silt away from the quay walls in the Floating Harbour and push it towards the sluices. When the deep sluice opened at low tide, a powerful undertow sucked the silt into the river to be carried away on the next tide. The shallow sluices enabled adjustment of the dock water level according to weather conditions.

Although this 'Underfall' system was rebuilt in the 1880s with longer sluices, Brunel's method of silt disposal is still in operation today. The silt is carried in mud barges or pumped to the sluices through a quayside pipe system from the more efficient modern 'Cutter-Suction' dredgers. These pipes and the underfall system can be seen today if you visit the Underfall Yard.

The problem of the sewage emptying into the Cut was finally solved a hundred years later with the completion of the sewerage and drainage system and foul water interceptors.

A Problem of Size: Brunel's Alterations

At the same time as he designed the Underfall system, Brunel also altered Jessop's entrance lock to the Cumberland Basin. This is where ships would wait for the tide to enter the harbour from the Bristol Channel.

By 1832, ships had become larger and Brunel's alteration of the entrance lock was once more not wide enough. A second change was needed so Brunel designed a new enlarged entrance lock to the south of the original. The innovative construction had floating iron caisson gates instead of the usual paired timber gates. It was crossed by a swing bridge, which Brunel insisted was made from tubular riveted iron girders, another of his progressive designs.

Later, in 1873, as ships grew bigger still, this entrance lock was enlarged again by the engineer Thomas Howard, so that it was now 350 feet long by 62 feet wide. Brunel's lock was dammed up. All three locks can be seen and visited today.

Jessop's enlarged Lock and Brunel's innovative southern lock; in the foreground is the the old Rownham Ferry.

A view of Bathurst Basin with a steam coaster about to enter the lock.
A tug is moored in the Avon New Cut. Further up river a steam packet awaits
passengers at the jetty by the new Bristol General Hospital .This was opened
in 1858 on the the site of John Acraman's Iron Works.

Bristol after the New Cut

The New Harbour

Taken as a whole, the system of the New Cut and Floating Harbour was an amazing feat of engineering and an incredible success. It hugely improved the docking arrangements; added about six miles of new wharf space; made loading and unloading cargo much safer and more efficient; and created opportunity for more industry and manufacturing, enabling Bristol to continue to develop as a port.

Although initially there were some teething problems with the harour, any loss of trade was reversed when the Bristol Corporation assumed control of the docks in 1848 and brought in the necessary changes and improvements. In 1873 the third much needed enlargement of the entrance lock from the Cumberland Basin took place. Then, over the next 30 years, fine granite quays were built along the harbour to replace the old wooden jetties and natural river banks. Gradually, new cargo handling facilities such as hydraulic and steam cranes were introduced and installed at the docks. Rail links were developed on both sides of the Floating Harbour, greatly increasing the efficiency of goods transit to and from the main railway network. More new buildings grew up: granaries, flour mills, factories and, later, the giant bond warehouses at Spike island and Ashton (now home to the Create Centre and a Storage business next to the Riverside Garden Centre). Then, in the late 19th century and early 20th century, the upper part of the docks (the original Frome Cut of 1240) was covered over to create what is now the city centre, leaving just Narrow Quay.

Throughout this time, sugar, tobacco, cotton, timber, sand, wine and wood pulp continued to arrive as bulk cargoes into the city docks and were taken by barge to factories along the Feeder Canal and elsewhere. Coal came from local coalfields that were developing nearby in Ashton, Bedminster and Southville. Chocolate, tobacco products, glass, soap, tanneries, printers and foundries continued as important manufacturing industries. And, of course, all the industries relevant to a busy port also flourished, from the shipyards where vessels were built and repaired to the coopers, or barrel makers, who supplied the containers for just about everything.

Early coal mining, hoisting coal from a shaft using a horse powered winding drum.

Recreational use of the harbour also developed during this time. Pleasure paddle steamers plied the waters of the harbour, taking people from the city centre to the Bristol Channel, South Wales and North Devon. The biggest firm was that of Peter and Alex Campbell, who moved their long established family steamer operations from the Clyde to the Bristol Channel in 1887. Over the next 80 years, their fleet was to take millions of passengers up and down the Channel, to every port and seaside town along the coast. Smaller steam launches took day-trippers to Hanham and Keynsham and sometimes to Bath for cream teas.

For about a hundred years after the opening of the new Cumberland Entrance Lock in 1873, Bristol harbour managed to continue as an incredibly busy place, with coastal and international trade still being brought right into the city centre. It is amazing to think of it as it was then, the ships sailing into the docks; the trade, the industry and the manufacturing; the sailors from all over the world; the accents and the colours; the smells and the noises: all right in the heart of the city.

Development of the Avon New Cut

Although the New Cut had originally been created to act as a tidal bypass to maintain the city's Floating Harbour, it soon developed significant navigation and industry in its own right.

The first ships to enter the harbour came up the New Cut and entered at the lock of Bathurst Basin because the Cumberland Basin locks were still unfinished. The Cut and the Bathurst entry

then continued to be used by smaller craft, and by schooners, ketches and barges being towed upriver by steam tugs. The earliest steam paddle packets taking passengers and goods to places such as Cork, South Wales and North Devon also used this route and moored up at the jetty by the General Hospital. One of them, The Velindra, is commemorated by the public house of the same name, that still exists close to the point where the steamers would have arrived and departed.

A tug approaching the Bathurst Basin lock passes the passenger paddle steamer Marchioness, departing the jetty by the Bristol General Hospital with the New Gaol to the left.

Industry also developed along the banks of the New Cut: ship building, tanneries, iron and zinc works and foundries, to name a few. In 1820, for example, an iron founder John Acraman opened a foundry at Bathurst Basin, on the site of the later General Hospital. The foundry specialised in anchors and chains and was one of the places that produced parts for Brunel's steamship the Great Western. Acraman's company went on to be involved in shipbuilding: first wood and iron vessels, and then vessels and floating bridges made entirely from iron. At one point, Acraman's was said to be the largest engineering firm in the world, employing 1,200 men.

New buildings also grew up on the Cut. The earliest major ones were those of the New Gaol, the remains of which can be seen on the corner of Cumberland Road and Wapping Road. The New Gaol was opened in 1820 on the the north bank of the New Cut when the notorious Newgate Prison in the city centre was closed. The new residents of Southville did not want the prison on their side, as it was being built at the same time as the fashionable houses on Coronation Road.

The 1820s and 1830s were troublesome times in Bristol, reflect-

The New Gaol showing the gate house and the governor's residence.

ing the poor economy of the country as a whole. Disturbances and riots were widespread as there was considerable poverty. The New Gaol represented to many the harsh rule of authority and the severe penalties meted out by the magistrates. The city was run by a self perpetuating council, unelected by its citizens, and it was not surprising that the situation culminated in an attack on what was seen as a symbol of oppression.

On the 24th of October 1831, the consecration of St Paul's Church on Coronation Road by the Bishop of Bath and Wells, (who had voted against the Reform Act in the House of Lords) sparked a protest by angry local people and he was driven off by a volley of stones and had to be protected. By the 29th of October, the disturbance had become a full blooded riot, with the Mansion House and most of Queens Square being set on fire. The Gaol was stormed by people wielding hatchets and sledge-hammers, the main door was smashed open and some 300 rioters poured in. 200 prisoners were released and the Governor's house was ransacked and set on fire. The chapel, the gallows and the dreaded treadmill were destroyed. Much of what was moveable was thrown into the New Cut and swept away with the ebbing tide.

Eventually, with the belated help of the militia, order was restored. 127 arrests were made of which 81 were found guilty and given sentences ranging from imprisonment to transportation. Four were sentenced to death and hanged publicly in front of a large crowd along Coronation Road on the 27th January 1832. The Gaol was repaired and used until 1883 but later demolished and sold to the Great Western Railway Company as a coalyard depot. The Gatehouse from which the executions took place is still in existence. Within the same year the Reform Bill was passed by parliament, giving a wider but limited enfranchisement to the population. A regular police force was formed and the East Street Police Station was the third to be built in Bristol. It is now part of a library, medical practice and housing complex.

An etching of the General Hospital shortly after it was opened in 1858.

Other notable buildings that grew up around the New Cut included the Bristol General Hospital, built in the 'warehouse' style on the Bathurst Basin in 1832. The basement of the building contained 8000 square feet of warehouse space, providing an income towards the hospital. For the patients above, "the fresh sea breezes blowing up the New Cut" were thought to be beneficial. Another note-worthy building, the Bathurst Hotel, appeared in 1830 and can still be seen today (it is now called The Louisiana).

The hotel and the basin were both named in honour of Charles Bragge Bathurst, MP for Bristol from 1796 to 1811.

New roads were constructed along the banks of the New Cut. Coronation Road was opened by the Dowager Lady Smyth in 1822 and it was about this time that the name Southville started to be used. Grand houses grew up along Coronation Road, York Road and Cumberland Road with many influential people living in the area. If we look at the list of names who requested, in March 1828, that St Paul's Church be built and look at the further list of those who attended the stone-laying ceremony 18 months later, we see mayors, sheriffs, Merchant Venturer officials, rich businessmen, solicitors, policy makers and several representatives and agents of European countries. For example, Sir A B Mascrenhas, Consul for Portugal, lived at Stroud Building on Coronation Road in 1833; and H Visger, Consul for Prussia, also lived in Coronation Road.

Later, in 1873, Alderman Proctor spent £500 to build 'Proctor's Walk' along the New Cut. He cleared weeds and bushes, put in trees, erected railings, and provided benches for people to enjoy the views. Many remnants of his 'boulevard' effect can still be seen today along Coronation Road: look out for fruit and ornamental trees amongst the jumble of green along the Cut and for the stone- built outlooks, which are too dangerous today to venture along.

At the Ashton end of the road, commanding great views of the bend on the river Avon, was Clift House. This was the dowager house for both Florence Upton and Dame Emily and was part of the Smyth Estate. Later, the house was to become a diphtheria hospital and was eventually demolished (the Riverside Garden Centre now stands on the same site). In 1882, the Smyth family donated some of the grounds of Clift House to the 'people of Bedminster' to make the first public park in Bristol. More land was added by Lady Smyth in 1902 and the name changed to Greville Smyth Park, a place we all still enjoy today.

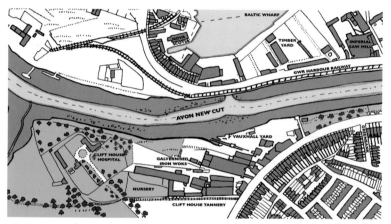

Clift House, the site of Vauxhall Pleasure Gardens, which provided entertainment for the people of Hotwells and Clifton during the mid 1700s

In 1896, the Great Western Railway Company built a railway line along the Cut, on the old towing path by Cumberland Road, to link the wharves on the northern and southern sides of the docks to the main rail network. The line was later extended and crossed over the Cut via a Swing Bridge built at Ashton in 1906.

Ashton, Bedminster and Southville

Up until the 17th century, the whole area south of the river had been entirely rural. Bedminster itself had long existed (as a settlement it was far older than Bristol), but it was still just a prosperous community clustered around the local parish church, set amongst fertile land. By the 1760s, it had become a sprawling and decaying market town, where orchards mixed with cottage industries and open land, but was still nothing like the place it is today. Although there were definitely dwellings on parts of the areas we now know of as Southville and Ashton, it was still mainly fields, meadows and hills. A stream called the Malago flowed down through Bedminster and joined the Avon at a site called Treen Mills (a set of mill ponds which were later enlarged to form the Bathurst Basin). All of the land came under the 'Manor of Bedminster' which had been bought by the Smyth family in 1605.

From the mid 18th century, however, the whole area began to change dramatically. Bristol coal was already being mined in Kingswood, but in 1748 the first mine-shaft was sunk in Bedminster, at South Liberty Lane. By the 1820s, not long after the New Cut was created, over a dozen coal pits were operating in the Bedminster and Ashton Vale coalfield, all to the financial benefit of the Smyth family. The largest of these was the Dean Lane pit (where Dame Emily Park is today). It employed over 400 men and even children as young as eight were working underground for 12 hours a day. The town of Bedminster was rapidly

DEAN LANE COLLIERY BEDMINSTER 1875

Winding gear

Engine house

Staith to carry drams from pithead to coal chutes

Slag heap

Coal chute

Coal chute

From this tiime, other new industries developed south of the river such as were foundries, smelting works, engineering works, tanneries, glue works, glass works and paint factories. A few of these industries were significant and worth mentioning in detail. John Acraman started the Gaol Ferry and opened large ironworks in 1820 on the site of the later General Hospital. The firm specialised in anchors and chains and produced parts for Brunel's S.S. Great Britain. Acraman later opened the Vauxhall shipyard on Coronation Road, named after the pleasure gardens that were once on that site. The yard was acquired by John Payne in 1862 and closed in 1924. Part of the slipway can still be seen today in the mud bank opposite the Underfall Yard. Frederick Braby

An 1827 illustration showing Bathurst locks and Acraman's iron works seen from the Floating Harbour.

transforming from a rural area to a mainly industrial one. It was now supplying a raw material – coal - for local industry, and it lay within easy access to the city docks, the new harbour and the growing city.

It is amazing to consider the transformation of the area after this point. Between 1801, just before the Cut was begun, and 1884, the population of Bedminster went from 3,000 to a staggering 78,000 as people poured in from depressed rural Somerset to come and work in the new industries. During these years, high-density terraced housing developed, mainly slums, where conditions were appalling and disease was rife.

opened up the Ashton Gate Iron and Zinc Works and the firm moved to its present site in Ashton in 1928.

Bristol has had a long and distinguished past regarding the production and sales of leather, with more leather being produced in Bristol than in the rest of the country. During the late 1800s Bristol had fourteen traditional tanneries plus others in the near vicinity; in 1883 six of these were sited in Bedminster. James Cox, born in 1807, was referred to as 'the tanner of Long Ashton'. He lived in the manor house in Nailsea where he bought his first tannery. He went into partnership with his brother Stephen. Cox Bros. continued to expand with a tannery in Yate but their main premises were on Coronation Road, a three and a half acre site at Clift House. The business was sold to Thomas Ware in 1878 and is now the only remaining tannery in Bristol.

Scraping the hides: part of the tanning process.

In the 1880s, E.S & A. Robinson's paper bag business and W. D & H. O. Wills' tobacco business both moved to new factories in Bedminster. These new industries generated considerable wealth for some, created thousands of new jobs for the poor and greatly added to the general prosperity of the area. By the early 20th century, Bedminster was a thriving suburb, with flourishing shopping centres on East Street, North street and West Street; packed churches and chapels; new schools, pubs and other public buildings.

Sporting events around the area of the New Cut are also well documented, with bare knuckle contests being fought outside the Ostrich Inn before the Bathurst Basin was excavated. Women as well as men took an active part in this sport and were described as being formidable. The boxer Billy Price, who fought as a young man at Bedmminster Arcade in the early 1930s, talked about the women wrestlers who were very popular. Here is a singular instance of higher pay for women as their bouts drew bigger crowds. Professional tournaments were being staged before capacity crowds at the Bristol South Baths right up to the 1950s.

Cricket and football were avidly played and followed in the area, with nearly every church and numerous firms having their own teams. Bristol City Football Club developed from an open field site recorded on a 1903 map with a tiny pavilion and two earth banks for spectators to view the game, a far cry from the fine stadium of today on the same site.

As a whole, Ashton, Bedminster and Southville had an incredible sense of community, something which still survives today. Thanks to the New Cut and Floating Harbour which geographically separated these areas from the rest of Bristol, they retained their distinct identity, dialect and local culture.

The Tide Changes

The New Cut and the Floating Harbour saved Bristol harbour from a fast decline and enabled the city's docks to continue and flourish for more than 150 years. It is very difficult to imagine what Bristol would be like today if this had not happened. However, no matter what improvements took place, Bristol was still an upriver port, and change was inevitable. The entry to the harbour might have been enlarged three times, but it still got to the point where it was not big enough for the largest ships of the day. The water between the Bristol Channel and the Cumberland Basin was difficult for these new vessels to navigate and there

were incidents of very serious groundings and mishaps amongst ships coming to the city. On March 31st 1857, for example, the three masted sailing vessel Mary Ann Peters was leaving the city docks, bound for West Africa, when she went aground by the old Rownham ferry and listed at an alarming angle as the tide ebbed. She was subsequently

A 1922 etching by Harry Banks. Discharging Cargo at the Grove.

refloated but many other vessels were not so fortunate. Well into the last century ships were regularly completely wrecked in this difficult reach of the Avon, blocking the river for other vessels and causing huge delays.

By the late 19th century, larger docks closer to the Bristol Channel were already being considered in order to cater for the bigger ships. In 1877 Avonmouth Dock was opened, situated on the north bank of the Avon; and in 1879, Portishead Dock (the one sketched out by Brunel) was opened on the North Somerset coast, only a mile or so from the mouth of the Avon. Both were linked by rail to Bristol and to the wider railway network and were able to handle ships of a much larger size without the dangers of a river journey. These docks began to handle bulk cargoes such as oil, grain, timber, sugar, coal and many other products that had been going into the city docks.

Despite Bristol's loss of the largest ships to these new ports, the city harbour remained vibrant right up until the late 1960s, as many Bristolians know and remember. However, changes in freight handling and containerisation led to a rapid decline at this point. Previously, goods had been moved in small containers such as baskets and sacks and this had required a large workforce. In the 1970s, however, the system was modernised and new, huge containers were introduced. This led to a complete change of cargo handling and a drastic reduction in the dock's workforce (something that happened in ports everywhere).

By the mid 1970s, many of the well known trading fleets had also disappeared from the city harbour and Bristol's own shipping company, the Bristol City Line, had come to an end after nearly a century of trading to New York. The paddle steamers too had closed, after 80 years of taking passengers on trips around the Bristol Channel. The last steam paddler of the fleet, the *Bristol Queen*, was sold for scrap in 1967.

Like so many other upriver ports, Bristol City Docks had finally succumbed to the rapid changes in ship sizes, infrastructure and handling. Motorways had killed off the coastal trade because goods could now be transported directly and quickly by road; and

roll-on roll-off ferries had added to the decline because motorways linked to the ferry ports and not to the old upriver ports. Coastal ports now handled most shipping trade, although in Bristol, sand and gravel dredged in the Bristol Channel were still being brought into the Floating Harbour until the 1990s; and some ship building on a much-reduced scale still took place on the Charles Hill shipyard site, now the Marina.

Along the New Cut, the decline in trade and traffic happened much earlier. By the 1930s, traffic was so reduced that the Ashton and Vauxhall swing bridges were fixed: it was no longer deemed viable to keep opening and closing them. Then, in the 1940s during World War II, both Totterdown and Bathurst locks were sealed off to try and ensure that the Luftwaffe had less chance of breaching the city docks, which was certainly their intention. Southville and Bedminster suffered a lot of damage, injury and death in the German attempt to destroy Bristol's docks and its infrastructure.

New Life for the Harbour

Despite being abandoned and neglected in the 1970s, Bristol's Floating Harbour had great potential for reinvention and for new life. People love to be near water and Bristolians and visitors to Bristol are no exception. Even at its lowest point, the regeneration of the harbour area had already begun, with the relocation of the Arnolfini and the arrival of the Watershed to Narrow Quay. Since then, the redevelopment of the area - sometimes controversial -

has once again returned the docks to the focal heart of the city and made them a catalyst for new enterprise and ideas.

Today, the Floating Harbour flourishes once again. Pleasure boats big and small are moored in the marina. Canoeing, sailing and rowing regularly take place. Ferries ply the waters once more with small trips around the harbour. Pleasure cruisers are back, with boats like the *Tower Belle* and the *Redshank* taking people on day cruises to Hanham and Keynsham; and the motor ship *Balmoral*, based in the docks, makes pleasure trips to various ports and seaside towns along the Bristol Channel. On an occasional basis, the harbour is visited by the Clyde based paddle steamer *Waverley*, the last oceangoing paddle steamer in the world.

New businesses, like the Lloyds Bank Headquarters, have been

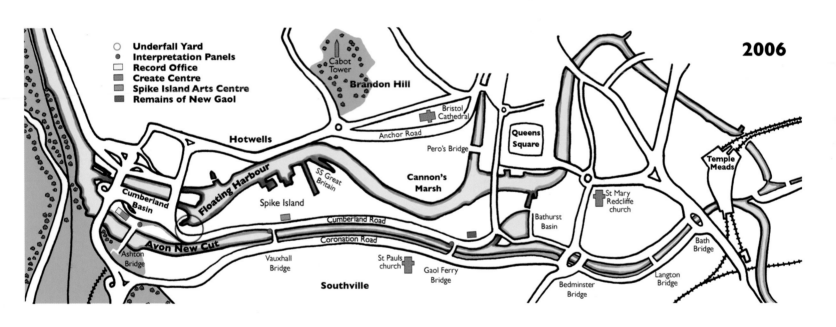

2006

- ○ Underfall Yard
- • Interpretation Panels
- ▢ Record Office
- ▣ Create Centre
- ▣ Spike Island Arts Centre
- ▣ Remains of New Gaol

Cabot Tower
Brandon Hill
Bristol Cathedral
Hotwells
Anchor Road
Pero's Bridge
Queens Square
Temple Meads
Floating Harbour
SS Great Britain
Cannon's Marsh
Cumberland Basin
Spike Island
St Mary Redcliffe church
Bathurst Basin
Cumberland Road
Avon New Cut
Coronation Road
Bath Bridge
Ashton Bridge
Vauxhall Bridge
St Pauls church
Gaol Ferry Bridge
Langton Bridge
Southville
Bedminster Bridge

St John's Church Bedminster was founded in late Saxon times and was an important ecclesiastical centre.

The rebuilding of St Mary's Redcliffe in the mid 14th century was in the new perpendicular style.

Queen Elizabeth I visited Bristol in 1574. As part of the festivities a mock fort was built and stormed for her entertainment.. The site is near Osborne Road, Southville.

On the completion of the Avon New Cut in 1809 a great feast was held. .

River Avon

Hotwells

Cumberland Basin

Floating Harbour

Floating Harbour

Spike Island

Avon New Cut

Ashton

Southville

During the Bristol Riots 29th & 30th October 1831 the New Gaol was stormed, parts of it set on fire and prisoners released.

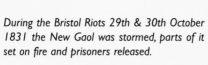

The earliest passenger steamers that sailed to Ireland, the West Country and Wales operated from the Avon New Cut.

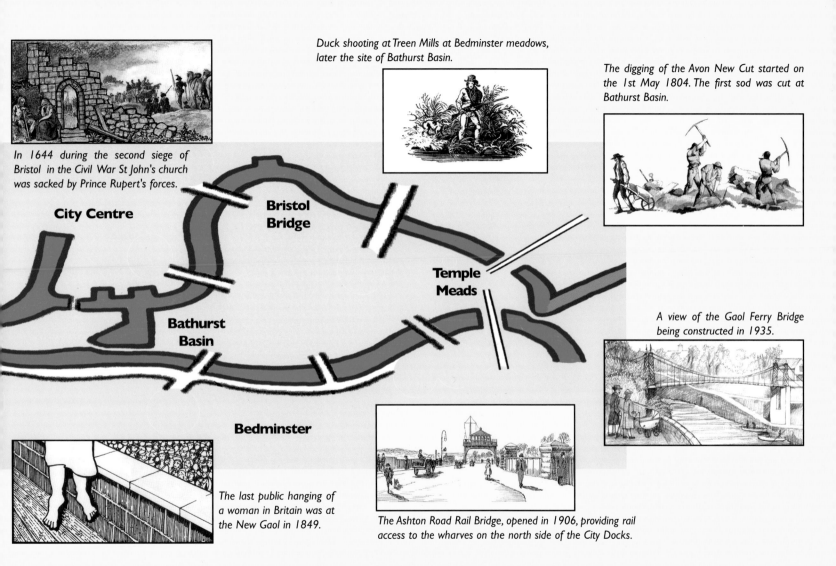

Duck shooting at Treen Mills at Bedminster meadows, later the site of Bathurst Basin.

The digging of the Avon New Cut started on the 1st May 1804. The first sod was cut at Bathurst Basin.

In 1644 during the second siege of Bristol in the Civil War St John's church was sacked by Prince Rupert's forces.

City Centre

Bristol Bridge

Temple Meads

Bathurst Basin

A view of the Gaol Ferry Bridge being constructed in 1935.

Bedminster

The last public hanging of a woman in Britain was at the New Gaol in 1849.

The Ashton Road Rail Bridge, opened in 1906, providing rail access to the wharves on the north side of the City Docks.

S. J. Loxton drawing of Ashton swing bridge and The Avon New Cut in full activity of shipping, rail and road traffic.

attracted to the shores of the Floating Harbour. Bars and restaurants line the banks of Narrow Quay, making it a vibrant place to socialise and relax. The presence of the Watershed and the Arnolfini centres make it a focus for the Arts in the city. In more recent years, new harbour-side apartments and living spaces have sprung up, making it a desirable place to live and work.

In a radically different way from its past existence, the Floating Harbour has once again become the centre of the city of Bristol.

This time it is a beautiful, lively, interesting centre for pleasure and leisure, for living and working. But it has not forgotten its roots. In the museums and heritage sites that can be visited along its banks - the Matthew, the SS Great Britain, the Industrial Museum, the Maritime Museum and the Underfall Yard. The history and heritage of the Floating Harbour is preserved, valued and celebrated as it should be. Overall, its future seems to be assured.

What of the Avon New Cut?

It is still essential to the city's docks and harbour: without it, they and everything they offer the city of Bristol would not be possible. However, apart from a few local devotees, it has remained largely neglected and unloved.

And yet, the New Cut is so important to the history and development of the city and the port of Bristol, as we have shown here; and it offers so much to anyone willing to explore it. In the following sections, you can read about some of the special features of the Avon New Cut: its churches and bridges; its geology, mud, wildlife, flora and fauna. We also look at what the future might hold for this amazing man-made channel and feat of engineering, flowing so close to where we live and work today.

Current day ferry taking commuters and visitors around the Floating Harbour.

A three masted barque 'hove to' awaits a pilot to take it up the Bristol Channel.

33

William Jessop

Born in Devon in 1745, William Jessop became a civil engineer specialising in the development of inland river works, harbours and canals. Bristol's Merchant Venturers accepted William Jessop's proposed designs for the development of the Floating Harbour and the construction of the Avon New Cut in 1803. Being over 60, William Jessop acted soley as arbitrator and consultant, while his son Josias was given the job of working on and over-seeing the Avon New Cut project.

William Jessop's father was a carpenter and shipwright who worked with John Smeaton on the Eddystone Lighthouse and they became firm friends. When he died he requested that John Smeaton become his son's guardian and take him on as apprentice. William was just sixteen. Starting as a draftsman, he went from assistant to deputy until Smeaton's retirement. It was hardly surprising that this apprenticeship with John Smeaton, the founding father of civil engineering, and his specialised training at the Smeaton Harbour Works led Jessop to become the greatest harbour engineer of his day. He designed and oversaw the building of three of the biggest dock systems in Bristol, Dublin and West India Dock in London. He was also responsible for a large number of both coastal and inland waterways that enhanced navigation and massively improved a number of drainage systems.

Jessop's method of working was to act initially as a consultant. He provided preliminary surveys by a landed surveyor or assistant engineer working under his direction. He then prepared the reports and estimates and gave his evidence to Parliament. From that point onwards he employed his skills as an engineer.

During his life he embraced and developed the new technologies of iron and steam. He designed and built cast-iron edge rails for a horse-drawn railway for coal wagons, possibly the world's first railway to be developed. He was also the first engineer to produce fully practical plans for steam draining fenlands. Therefore, as a professional civil engineer and forerunner to Brunel, Jessop's importance can hardly be exaggerated. As a man, he was modest and self-effacing, never failing to act with the highest professional integrity; a kind man to colleagues and juniors. He trained, inspired and worked with many engineers, for example Benjamin Outram, Ralph Walker and four of his own sons, the most notable of whom was his second son Josias.

Along with his wife, he raised eight children without a single infant death. This was a rare achievement for the 18th century. where the norm for child mortality was extremely high, due to bad sanitation, poverty and ignorance.

Jessop lived a full and active life. As well as being an engineer, he also held the office of Mayor of Newark twice and was elected

Alderman. He reorganised the Society of Civil Engineers in 1793 and became Justice of the Peace in 1805. He finally died in 1814 at the grand age of 69.

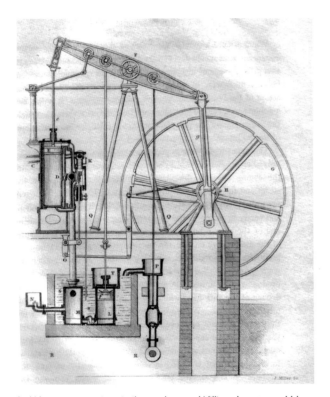

An early Watt steam engine similar to the type William Jessop would have used to lift the spoil from the bed of the New Cut.

Isambard Kingdom Brunel

When he died in 1859, at the modest age of 53, Isambard Kingdom Brunel left behind a civil engineering legacy that is still apparent today, some two hundred years after his birth. Known as the 'Little Giant' this dynamic Victorian, traditionally pictured in a high beaver hat, hands in pockets and smoking a cigar, gave us a host of new railways, bridges, docks and steamers, many of which are still in full service.

Isambard's father, Sir Marc Brunel, was also an engineer and worked on projects as varied as a stocking-knitting machine and a floating landing stage. He cultivated his son's early talent for observation and drawing, added technical training in France and then took him on as an assistant in the construction of the Thames Tunnel. On that difficult and troubled project the young Brunel showed both practical skills and, when the river inundated the works in 1828, great bravery.

While recovering in Bristol from injuries received in the tunnel, Isambard Brunel heard of a plan to build a bridge over the Avon Gorge. He promptly submitted his ideas for a graceful suspension bridge to the committee appointed to choose the best proposal. Although placed second in the final design competition Brunel burst in upon the judges and by sheer force of argument persuaded them to choose his own scheme.

Work on the Clifton Suspension Bridge began in June 1831, but was halted four months later by riots in the city following the failure of the Reform Bill. Brunel took his part in restoring law and order by becoming a special constable and later appeared as a witness in the ensuing inquiries into the devastating Bristol Riots. However, the events of 1831 affected both the bridge project and Brunel's report on improvements in the Bristol docks.

By the time Brunel married Mary Horsley in 1836 his career, which was vitally important to him, was back on course. Work on the bridge had resumed to the point where he was able to cross the Gorge in a basket and, more importantly, he had been chosen as the engineer for the infant Great Western Railway. Beginning with a survey of every inch of the route from London to Bristol, he was to become a pivotal figure, defending the proposals in the Parliamentary process, designing most of the works and equipment and overseeing the massive task of construction. Like George Stephenson, Brunel gathered his own team of assistants around him, but did a staggering amount of work himself, travelling in his own design of carriage and writing countless detailed notes to be stuck in his hat as reminders or passed on for action.

Brunel's choice of a 7ft broad gauge for the new railway may have

been too visionary and his ideas for locomotives had to be revised by Daniel Gooch, but the line from London to Bristol, opened throughout in 1841, was a magnificent achievement. It included a radical new bridge at Maidenhead, a deep cutting at Sonning and the magnificent Box Tunnel, through which the sun is said to shine end to end only on Brunel's birthday. The smooth 125mph ride of today's trains owes much to Isambard Kingdom Brunel and his choice of an easily-graded route.

The GWR scheme was a springboard for more Brunel involvement in railway extensions westwards. His vision saw these as part of an international route from the magnificent station at Paddington right through to New York and his first steamer, the 1,340 ton SS Great Western, was built for just this purpose. The SS Great Britain, later to be rescued from its grave in the Falkland Islands and brought home for restoration, and the huge 18,915 ton SS Great Eastern were to follow.

Brunel had incredible versatility and imagination. He suggested a canal through the Panama isthmus; designed a combination gunboat and tank landing craft; and conceived a thoroughly novel yet practical design for a huge hospital that could be prefabricated in England and shipped out to Renkioi in Turkey to cater for casualties in the Crimean War. He was deeply involved in everything he did, including a physical confrontation with a contractor and his men working on the Oxford, Worcester & Wolverhampton Railway. More personal was the equipment he devised to dislodge a coin he had swallowed while entertaining his children with party tricks. It involved a board that would turn him upside down and forceps for use by his surgeon brother-in-law to attempt the extraction.

For the Cornwall Railway Brunel, devised a special design for the 34 trestle timber bridges needed to get from the Tamar to Truro. Across the Tamar itself his Saltash Bridge revealed his great ingenuity, including the use of rising tides to raise the spans into position. But, drained by this, countless other projects and the enormous effort he had put into the SS Great Eastern, Brunel became a sick man and saw the completed bridge only from a couch on a flat truck. After recuperation a final effort secured the completion of his great vessel but a lifetime of intense work proved too much and brought on a stroke. Finally at his home in London in July 1859, this remarkable man passed away.

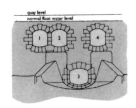

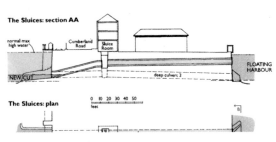

The Brunel scraper boat BD6 at work in the Cumberland Basin in the 1950s. Built in 1843 it was eventually retired in 1961.

The Sluices
"These are under 'A' block on the Cumberland Rd boundary and are still operated almost daily to adjust the dock water levels after rainfall. Although now automated, the process still requires vigilance from the docks engineer and his staff. The original cast iron sluice paddles have recently been renewed and one of the old paddles is displayed outside 'A' block".

Bridges

Bath and Bedminster Bridges

These two cast iron bridges were built by the Coalbrookdale Company in 1805. In 1806, one iron bridge on Hills Bridge (Bath road) collapsed whilst under construction, killing two men.

A fault in the design was suspected, but the bridge was rebuilt with no structural changes. This survived until March 1855, when a steam barge delivering coke to the railway works struck the ribs of the bridge, causing it to collapse completely. According to an eyewitness, it came down like a pack of cards leaving nothing standing; two more lives were lost.

A temporary footbridge was erected by June and a road bridge before the end of 1855, which was eventually replaced by a wider one in 1909.

Bedminster Bridge By S. J. Loxton.

Harford's (Bedminster) Bridge was built to the same design and, although shaken by a collision, it lasted until it was pulled down in 1882. It was then replaced by the current bridge, which is at least three times the previous width.

Langton Street Bridge

This footbridge was originally erected as a temporary bridge on the site where Bedminster bridge now stands, while the New Cut work was in process. It was then transported on barges at full tide and sited at Langton Street. It is currently known as the Banana Bridge because of its shape and has recently been painted a complimentary yellow colour.

Gaol Ferry Bridge

John Acraman established the Wapping Gaol ferry in 1829; and took its name from the New Bristol Gaol nearby. Passengers walked down the steep stone-paved slipways which are still visible today. The ferry carried foot passengers at a cost of 1/2 d per passenger, carrying approximately 10,000 people every week. The rights of the ferry were transferred to the City Corporation in 1854, which continued to operate the ferry until

1934, when it was closed because it was losing money. It could not operate at low tide without extensive dredging of the New Cut. The large slip under Coronation Road was used as a quay, with a small shop in the tunnel under the road.

In 1935 a contract was given to David Rowell & Co. Ltd. of London to construct a suspension footbridge at a cost of £2,564. This is now the main pedestrian bridge linking Southville and Bedminster with the City Centre.

Vauxhall Bridge

Vauxhall ferry was established in the 1860s for people to cross the New Cut, from Hotwells at the Overfall Dam to Clift house and gardens on the Southville side. It was later moved upstream near the site of the present bridge, due to an accident in 1894 in which two people were drowned.

Vauxhall Bridge was built as a swing bridge over the New Cut in the closing years of the 19th century. Boats and barges travelling up the New Cut entered the upper part of the floating Harbour via Bathhurst lock and Basin. Local traffic used this bridge to cross between Bedminster and Hotwells.

The bridge was officially opened and named by the Lady Mayoress, Lady Ashman, with a silver key on the 1st of June 1900. Shipping traffic in the New Cut dwindled very rapidly in the 1920s but occasional use continued until 1935, when an order was obtained "to close the bridge permanently to all shipping traffic." The machinery and resting pontoon for the swing-bridge were removed, leaving it as a static footbridge.

Ashton Rail and Road Swing Bridge

Ashton Road/Rail Bridge was probably unique: a two decked swing bridge with the road above and the railway below, it was erected in 1906 by a local firm J.Lysaught at a cost of £70,389.
River traffic was controlled by cones fixed to a mast on the super-structure. The railway (for goods only) was an extension of the Bristol Harbour railway, which had been built from Temple meads to Wapping wharf in 1872. This extension passed under

Cumberland Road along the Cut and across the new bridge to join the Portishead and Ashton line.
During the 1950s the bridge became fixed and the superstructure removed. The remainder of the harbour railway closed in 1964. Records from 1907-8 show that the bridge opened to shipping on average 10 times a day.

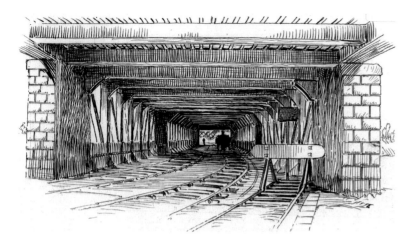

The Loxton illustration above shows the lower railway deck of Ashton Swing Bridge in operation. Below as it is today, part of the Sustrans cycle track.

Churches

St Luke's Church

St Luke's church, designed by John Norton, was built during 1860-61 and was located on York Road, Bedminster.
The original church tower at the northwest corner had four angle

pinnacles (which were sadly removed in alterations by P Hartland Thomas in 1933). The interior was fairly bare being "low church in rite". Over the door was the inscription "the poor have gospel preached unto them".

In the early 1860s, Princes Street behind York Road was an appalling slum and became the focus of David Dowdney, the great reforming clergyman. He came to St Luke's when it was first built and stayed for 30 years. He was a towering figure who did all he could to help the poor. He became well known for his soup kitchen, Bible reading and mission hall.

The mission hall is still there in William Street, behind the Blind Institute; it is a curious building and is currently a warehouse. New flats built in 2006 have been given the name Dowdney Court. The church was closed in 1968 and demolished 1970. There is now a petrol filling station on the site.

Church of the Vow

Zion House on Coronation Road was originally the Church of the Vow and was a non-conformist chapel. Its origin lies with the story of John Hare, who came to Bristol from Somerset in the 17th century to make his fortune. He was a young man of 15 who would have walked or had a lift in a hay wain arriving in Bristol late at night. Being penniless and having no friends or relatives, he climbed over a wall to sleep. When he awoke he thought that he was in heaven as the wall he had climbed over had taken him into a cherry orchard. It was a sunny May morning and the trees were in full blossom. Looking up at the blue sky and white blossom he

Zion Chapel by Samuel Coleman

made a vow that once he had made his fortune he would build a temple on this spot.

John Hare did make a fortune in linoleum and similar products and did indeed build the temple. However, by this time the New Cut had been dug and the orchard had disappeared, so he built his church on another site close by. The church became a congregational church and its fine interior and best features have been retained. It's currently used as a housing office.

St Paul's Church

Early in 1829, land called "three acre ground" was purchased from John Acraman to build a church to accommodate the increasing population of Southville. The foundation stone was laid on 8th September. The Bishop of Bath and Wells came to consecrate the church in 1831. When he arrived, his carriage was showered with mud and stones by an angry crowd, who were voicing their objection to his decision to vote against the Reform Act. This event took place only days before the Bristol riots.

St Paul's became a parish church in 1852 and was enlarged and re-consecrated with accommodation for 750. The church was a central focus for social activities and organised societies, providing help and support to the poorer members of the congregation. It was partly destroyed during the Second World War in bombing raids and was rebuilt in 1958.

St Raphael's

In August 1854, Rev. Robert Miles, Rector and fourth son of P. J. Miles of Leigh Court, purchased a piece of ground fronting the New Cut. His wish was to build a church for the use of seaman using the port and an alms house for the widows of sailors.

The Rev. A. H. Ward became vicar of this unconsecrated church. The services he held were conducted using high church practice, which were a rejection of the Protestant element in favour of the reformation Catholic traditions. These views caused bitter controversy. By 1878 the Bishop of Bristol could no longer accept Rev. Ward's continued high church services, as such practices were against the wishes of the protestant church and were known as "Spikey". An uppity priest was therefore a "spike" which is one of the stories behind the name of Spike Island.

The view below shows St Raphael's church from the Floating Harbour with the Fairburn steam crane which is still functional and operated occasionally by the Industrial Museum.

The church was consecrated on the 30th May 1893 and became a parish church. It was later destroyed during the bombing of Bristol in 1940. All that remains is an entrance way between the new blocks of flats, down river from Gaol Ferry Bridge.

Geology of the Cut

The geology of the Bristol area can be divided into two broad types of rocks. There are the very old rocks which underlie the whole area which are of Carboniferous age and older (400 million years). These are overlain by a series of comparatively younger rocks of Triassic and Jurassic age (around 200 to 135 million years old).

The older rocks consist of two main types around the city of Bristol; the hard grey limestones of the Downs, the Mendips and the Avon Gorge which are often deformed and folded, as seen in the dipping beds near the Suspension Bridge. On top of these lie the coal measures and the pennant sandstones. In many areas, these older rocks are exposed at the surface but in some areas, they are overlain by the younger Triassic series of rocks which are generally flat-lying or gently dipping and consist of sandstones, clays and younger, softer limestones (e.g. Bath Stone). The Triassic rocks seen in the Cut are Bunter sandstones laid down in desert conditions and interestingly, this porous sandstone is the reservoir rock for most of the gas fields in the Southern North Sea. There is a missing section of rock between the older and younger rocks (called an unconformity) where sediments were either not laid down or were eroded away before the newer rocks were deposited very much later. The Cut consists exclusively of the younger series; the older ones lying buried much deeper down.

The western end of the Cut has been dug from very recent soft alluvium deposited by the Avon in the last one million years. Moving further east, a bed of harder sandstone about half a metre thick can be seen to emerge on the north side by the Spike Island Arts Centre. This is the youngest (top) section of the series of Bunter sandstone beds which are separated by softer shale layers (compact clay). The land starts to rise slightly approaching the railway bridge on Cumberland Road as the gently arched beds of Triassic sandstone are in evidence on either side. These are made up of reddish brown sandstone, up to 3 – 4 metres thick, with soft shale in between. In places, the shale layer has been supported by masonry to prevent erosion.

A good vantage point from which to identify these features is Gaol Ferry Bridge, where it is evident that the rocks must be quite hard to support the vertical rock walls. The Bunter sandstone terminates fairly abruptly just to the east of the bridge, before disappearing and being replaced by alluvium. This much softer material has allowed the Bathurst Basin to be excavated between the Docks and the Cut. From here to Bedminster Bridge, the banks lie at a shallow angle due to the presence of the softer material. Close to the bridge buttresses have been constructed to allow the bridge to span a narrower gap.

The red Triassic sandstone reappears beneath Bedminster Bridge as it makes up the high ground of Redcliff Hill and Redcliff Parade and it is this characteristic coloured stone that gives this area its name. The Cut has been dug into the red sandstone which can be seen close to the water at low tide between Bedminster Bridge and Bath Bridge; however, the banks have been sloped back into the overlying alluvium.

Mud, Glorious Mud.

The mud in the New Cut mostly originated upstream. All rivers wash earth from their banks with slow flowing rivers carrying more earth than water. The soil washed down from the land over which the River Avon and its tributaries flow, ends up finally in the sea, but on the way some of it rests in the Cut. The mud is moved by the twice-daily ebb and surge of the tide and more is added by the ingenious transfer of silt from the City Docks via the Underfall (one of Brunel's clever ideas). Small additions come from the continuous erosion of the rock walls of the Cut itself.

As well as washing soil away, the river deposits mud in the slowest flowing parts, so that banks gradually build up. These banks are regularly immersed in brackish water and so become home to plants and micro-organisms which can tolerate salt.

During the warmer months marine plants flourish at the water margins. Some of these are the familiar sea

asters, scurvy grass or other large plants but there are also many different types of microscopic plants. All of these plants convert carbon dioxide into plant tissue as they grow, using energy from the sun and locking carbon emissions from the atmosphere. Mud banks are very fertile and can produce twice the plant growth of the same area of field.

This phenomenal growth takes place at the top surfaces of the mud. Beneath this there are layers of decaying matter and the micro-organisms that feed on it, producing the characteristic smell. Larger organisms such as nematode worm, feed on these tiny but extremely nutritious micro-organisms and in turn the worms and small crustaceans are eaten by fish and birds. Without the mud we would not have the fish and bird life which characterises the New Cut.

There are benefits too for the land near the water, as the nutrients produced in the mud are distributed in the remains of the muddy meals of the Cut's wildlife.

In other cultures and in times past the usefulness of mud was more appreciated. It can be used to make buildings and pottery for instance. Some local potters have been experimenting with mud from the New Cut which produces beautiful subtle coloured glazes of green, blue and brown.

Richard Long, the world famous Bristol artist, has produced lovely artwork with mud and the mud itself also looks very beautiful, as local photographers have shown. W. M. Turner (who painted The Fighting Temeraire and other well known studies of light and water) is reputed to have said " Give me mud and I will

show you gold" referring to the reflections of sunlight on mudflats.

Other uses of mud include medicinal use as the smelly richness can provide dietary supplements not easily obtained otherwise, but the waters of the Cut are likely still to be too polluted for this to be recommended. There is no reason why mud baths from the Cut could not be just as efficacious as those from Dead Sea mud.

Bath bricks made of dried mud, which were invemted by Mr Bath of Bridgewater, were a kind of abrasive used as a cleaner and probably more environmentally friendly than many modern cleaning compounds.

Next time you walk by the Cut, take a good look at the mud, you may learn to love this "bread and butter" of the wildlife!

Wildlife

This tidal waterway is a valuable wildlife corridor and a source of enjoyment for people living in the centre of Bristol. We hope to protect and increase wildlife habitats in Southville, Bedminster and Ashton. It has now become an area rich in flora and fauna - a green lung in the centre of the city.

Birds

Over 30 species of birds have been seen along the Cut, including the Grey Heron and the Cormorant. Both of these birds eat fish from the Cut, their presence being an indicator of the health of the waterway.

The Cormorant

The Cormorant is a large dark, almost black sea-bird which catches fish and eels by swimming powerfully under water. It can consume its own weight of fish in a day. The cormorant needs to stretch out its wings to dry and to oil its feathers from a gland near the base of its tail, as it lacks the waterproof feathers of other water birds.

The Grey Heron

The Grey Heron is a regular visitor to the Cut and with its long legs and pick-axe bill is easily recognised. It is a solitary feeder, usually standing motionless in shallow water where it will strike swiftly for fish, eels, and frogs. Herons nest together in a heronry, usually in tall trees. There is a nearby heronry at Eastwood Farm, St Annes.

The Common Sandpiper

The Common Sandpiper is a small wading bird, the size of a starling. It has a high piping call and flies low over the water with pointed and drooping wings. It feeds along the Cut on the outgoing tide on insects, worms and small crustaceans that it finds in the mud. When on the ground it has a distinctive head-bobbing motion.

The Black Headed Gull

Of several species of gull seen on the Cut, the Black Headed Gull is easily distinguished by its red legs and beak. In spring it has a dark chocolate brown head (not black) which turns to white in the autumn. Its call is much higher pitched than the larger gulls and has a somewhat peevish sound.

The Mallard

The Mallard, a well-known and most handsome duck, is rarely absent from the Cut. The drake has a glossy green head and purple wing patch. The duck lays between 7-16 eggs, quite often in gardens adjacent to the Cut. The drake takes no part in rearing the ducklings, which are vulnerable to predators, especially the larger gulls. Despite this, the mallard population is flourishing.

Wild Flowers

Over 90 species of flowering plants are present between Gaol Ferry Bridge and Ashton Bridge

Ivy Broomrape

The rare Ivy Broomrape is special to the Avon New Cut and found only in a very few other habitats. It is a parasite growing from the roots of ivy plants. It has a yellowish-purple stem and creamy flowers in summer; the flowers last for a short time in June but you will be able to see the fruiting stalks for several months. This plant is the emblem of the group FrANC, Friends of the New Cut.

The Spindle

The Spindle is a small multi-branched tree or shrub with yellowish-green flowers and fruit capsules that are bright pink, splitting open when ripe to reveal orange seeds. Its wood provides spindles for spinning or can be used for artists' charcoal.

Purple Toadflax

Purple Toadflax grows alongside the railway line, especially on the north bank of the Avon Cut. It is often found on waste ground and will even grow out of walls. It has small purple flowers with a spur arranged in a spikelet. It flowers from June to August.

Sea Aster is a tall plant with fleshy leaves which grows on the mud banks. It has a daisy-like flower with a yellowish centre and pale purple petals in summer.

Common Scurvy Grass has white flowers from April to August and is found overhanging the banks or growing out of the mud, like the sea aster. They both can withstand being covered by the brackish or salty water of the Avon New Cut.

Some of the more common wild flowers to look out for along the New Cut

Traveller's Joy, a climbing plant whose small greenish-cream flowers attract bees. Sometimes called The Old Man's Beard because of the masses of feathery fruits that appear in the autumn.
<

Hemp Agrimony, which has small pinkish flowers arranged in clusters from June to September.

Teasel, a tall plant with tough, prickly, hollow stems. The flower heads often remain throughout the winter, providing food for birds.
<

Chicory, a tall plant with attractive blue flowers. Its roots can be roasted and ground to add to some kinds of coffee.

Alexanders, a tall plant with dark green shiny leaves and yellow flowers from April to June.

Lesser Celandine grows near to the ground and has yellow flowers that brighten up the spring months.

Trees

Over 30 species of trees can be seen along the Cut, including one or two fig trees which are believed to have grown from fruits discarded by passing sailors in times gone by.

Common Lime
Has wonderful sweet-smelling yellowish-white flowers in early summer and small round green fruit in the autumn. Its inner bark can be used to make matting and ropes.

Whitebeam
Has striking leaves green above and a profusion of downy white hairs on the underside. White flowers bunched in flattish heads and clusters of scarlet berries when ripe.

Cherry
Cherry trees grow on the banks adjacent to Coronation Road, producing a flush of white blossom in April / May. The red edible fruit ripens during the summer and is enjoyed by both birds and people.

Wild Apple
Are small trees with white to red fragrant blossom. Their apples are quite variable sometimes yellow, green or red. The fruit are edible but not always pleasant as they can be extremely bitter.

Hawthorn
Hawthorn trees and shrubs are often found in hedgerows. Their distinctive white blossom produces red berries (haws) in the autumn. The haws provide birds with food during the winter, and the hawthorn wood can be used to make walking sticks.

London Plane
Tall broad-leaved London Plane are common to urban environments as they regularly shed their bark and are therefore highly resiliant to pollution. They give Coronation Road and Commercial Road the structure of "the boulevard' intended by Alderman Proctor when planting along the Avon New Cut in 1873.

Butterfly Junction

Over 19 species of butterfly and day moth have been spotted on this abandoned industrial site which is covered with a mix of bramble, grasses and buddleia.

During the summer months a variety of grasses provides an abundant breeding ground for several species like the Marbled White, Ringlet and Skippers. The Common Blue mainly breeds on Bird's-foot Trefoil, a low lying plant with small slipper like yellow flowers.

Meadow Brown

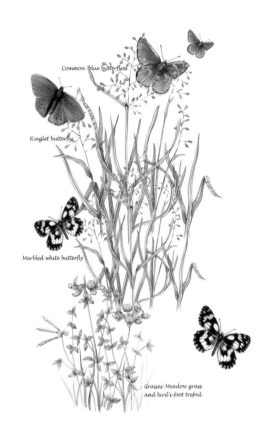

Common blue butterflies

Ringlet butterfly

Marbled white butterfly

Grasses: Meadow grass and bird's-foot trefoil

More common butterflies like the Tortoiseshell, Red Admiral and Peacock regularly pass through the site to feed or rest. Rarer visitors include Small Copper, Orange-tip and migrants such as Painted Lady and Clouded Yellow also visit butterfly junction.

The site is regularly monitored and maintained to encourage the grasses and keep the more invasive plants under control by a group of dedicated local residents and organisations.

The site also provides a safe home for a variety of grasshoppers and crickets along with beetles and other insects.

Red Admiral

The Future of the Avon New Cut

What do we think that local people will want the Cut to be in the future?

Perhaps it could be a part of bustling, waterfront Bristol, full of bars and restaurants, with flats built on any pieces of land that are big enough. There could be suspended walkways over the water, a dam maybe, to create a huge enclosed lake.

Or would we rather have a romantically neglected Cut with crumbling walls and bridges, a place where wildlife abounds and people rarely venture?

Ideas for improvements range from the totally impractical (remove the mud), through the very expensive (suspended walkways and pontoon bridges) to simple and relatively cheap conservation.

There is potential for the use of the water itself to grow and as long as anglers and boat users are sensitive to the needs of wild life this could enhance the amenity of the Cut. Small craft, moving relatively slowly, would bring back some of the old lively use of the water and look attractive. The water flows very strongly at some states of the tide, which could provide challenging and exciting water sports. Access to the water is muddy and difficult at present but could be improved perhaps by the installation of one or two small piers.

A windmill or two may also add to the attractiveness of the area while generating green energy and it may also be possible to harness the tidal flow with water turbines.

Conservation of this beautiful feature of Bristol could include clearing the banks of rubbish and this is already being carried out occasionally by groups of volunteers. Cutting down dead trees and planting different and more appropriate species has also begun. A start has been made to reduce the noise and danger from speeding traffic near the Cut, again at the instigation of local people.

Proposals to improve access will need to be balanced against disturbance to wild life. The tides and salt marshes, the birds, insects and flowers and the wildness of this serene environment are the features which local people love about the Cut and minimal change may be the best way to preserve these.

Friends of the Avon New Cut (FrANC)

Residents of South Bristol wishing to protect and promote enjoyment of the Cut have formed a group known as Friends of the Avon New Cut. This new group joins others such as the Malago Valley Conservation Group, which promote and protect local waterways. The group recognises that the Cut is a significant wildlife corridor into the centre of the city, and is seeking to have it registered as a designated wildlife site. FrANC has already produced a leaflet called Discovering Wildlife on the Avon New Cut and has plans to install interpretation boards and appropriate artwork alongside the New Cut.

A Final Thought

As a result of this book and the story it tells, we very much hope that you too will want to explore and enjoy the Avon New Cut. We also hope you will want to help ensure that its heritage, its significance and its wildlife are not forgotten by the people of Bristol.

Bibliography

Ref no BRO PBA /crp/r/1/1
I K Brunels reports
31 8 1832

Industrial Archaeology of the Bristol Region
Angus Buchanan & Neil Cossons, David and Charles

The Great Iron Ship
James Dugan Sutton publishing

William Jessop Engineer
A W Skempton, Charles Hadfield + Portrait 1805

Bedminster The Archive Photograph Series
Anton Bantock and members of the Malago Society
Tempus publishing ltd

Southville People and Places
C.L.A.S.S
Fiducia Press

Bristol a People's History
Peter Aughton
Carnegie publishing ltd

The Book of Trades (1835)
published by Thomas Tegg

Century Magazine (1881-1882)
F Warne & Co

Malogo society Magazines

Web Sites

Bristol and Slavery:
http://www.headleypark.bristol.sch.uk/slavery/main.htm
Bristol docks:
http://en.wikipedia.org/wiki/Bristol_Harbour
http://www.farvis.com/harbour.htm
http://www.farvis.com/Brunel's%20locks.htm
http://www.underfallboatyard.co.uk/history.htm
http://www.cotch.net/River_Avon
http://www.hotwell-press.co.uk/press/bharbourside/harbbrfhist.html

200th celebration of the Avon New Cut was marked by 2 bridge crossings organised by the Sustainable Southville Group.